MY BEST FRIEND IS OUT OF THIS WORLD

by Sarah Albee
illustrated by Nate Evans

My name is Maddy.
I have a best friend
named Victor.

Dear Parent:

Buckle up! You are about to join your child on a very exciting journey. The destination? Independent reading!

Road to Reading will help you and your child get there. The program offers books at five levels, or Miles, that accompany children from their first attempts at reading to successfully reading on their own. Each Mile is paved with engaging stories and delightful artwork.

Getting Started
For children who know the alphabet and are eager to begin reading
- easy words • fun rhythms • big type • picture clues

Reading With Help
For children who recognize some words and sound out others with help
- short sentences • pattern stories • simple plotlines

Reading On Your Own
For children who are ready to read easy stories by themselves
- longer sentences • more complex plotlines • easy dialogue

First Chapter Books
For children who want to take the plunge into chapter books
- bite-size chapters • short paragraphs • full-color art

Chapter Books
For children who are comfortable reading independently
- longer chapters • occasional black-and-white illustrations

There's no need to hurry through the Miles. Road to Reading is designed without age or grade levels. Children can progress at their own speed, developing confidence and pride in their reading ability no matter what their age or grade.

So sit back and enjoy the ride—every Mile of the way!

For my own little space invaders
S.A.

For Kurt Liesner, Jerry Moon,
Jeff Beith, and Peter Martin—thanks
for the years of friendship
N.E.

Library of Congress Cataloging-in-Publication Data
Albee, Sarah.
My best friend is out of this world / by Sarah Albee ; illustrated by Nate Evans.
    p.   cm. — (Road to reading.   Mile 2)
Summary: When Maddy invites her best friend, Victor, over for dinner, her parents
are shocked to discover that he is a space alien.
ISBN 0-307-26202-2 (pbk.)
[1. Extraterrestrial beings—Fiction. 2. Friendship—Fiction.]
I. Evans, Nate, ill. II. Title. III. Series.
PZ7.A3174   My 1998
[E]—dc21   98-12754
                                                                        CIP
                                                                        AC

A GOLDEN BOOK • New York
Golden Books Publishing Company, Inc. New York, New York 10106

ISBN: 0-307-26202-2

A MCMXCVIII

This afternoon
I called him up.
"Come to dinner tonight,"
I said.
"My dad is cooking meatloaf."

"Meatloaf!" said Victor.
"I will be right over."

The doorbell rang.

My mother opened the door.

"How do you do,
Mrs. Wilson?" said Victor.
Victor is very polite.

"These are for you," he said.

"Flowers," said my mother.

"How nice."

"Come on, Victor,"
I said.
"Let's play in my room."

We played beauty parlor.

We played video games.
I won every time.

I showed him
my pet snake.

He showed me
his cool new shoes.

"Dinner!" called my father.

We went downstairs.

"Oh, boy," said Victor.

"Meatloaf!"

We ate dinner.

Then Victor said,

"I have a big surprise!"

"My tooth came out!"
he said.

"Your tooth," said my father.
"How nice."

After dinner,
we played in the sandbox.

We played ball
until it got dark.

Then Victor called his mother.

She came to pick him up.

"Thank you for dinner,
Mr. and Mrs. Wilson,"
said Victor.
"My mom says next time
Maddy must come
to our house!"

I waved good-bye
to Victor.
Off he went.

Maybe tomorrow
I will invite
my friend Stacey over.